NO BAD BEARS

NO
BAD
BEARS

OPHELIA'S
BOOK OF MANNERS

MICHELE DURKSON CLISE

WITH JONATHAN ETRA

VIKING

For my mother, Thelma Louise, who
taught me to be a good little bear

———————— ℭ ————————

VIKING

Published by the Penguin Group

Viking Penguin, a division of Penguin Books USA Inc.,
375 Hudson Street, New York, New York 10014, U.S.A.
Penguin Books Ltd, 27 Wrights Lane, London W8 5TZ, England
Penguin Books Australia Ltd, Ringwood, Victoria, Australia
Penguin Books Canada Ltd, 10 Alcorn Avenue, Toronto, Ontario, Canada M4V 3B2
Penguin Books (N.Z.) Ltd, 182–190 Wairau Road, Auckland 10, New Zealand

Penguin Books Ltd, Registered Offices: Harmondsworth, Middlesex, England

First published in 1992 by Viking Penguin, a division of Penguin Books USA Inc.

3   5   7   9   10   8   6   4   2

Text copyright © Michele Durkson Clise, 1992
Illustrations copyright © Marsha Burns, 1992
All rights reserved

LIBRARY OF CONGRESS CATALOGING-IN-PUBLICATION DATA
Clise, Michele Durkson.
No bad bears : Ophelia's book of manners /
by Michele Durkson Clise.
p.   cm.
Summary: Ophelia and her teddy bear friends provide
instructions in etiquette.
ISBN 0-670-83883-7
1. Etiquette for children and teenagers.
[1. Etiquette.] I. Title.
BJ1857.C5C46   1992
395′.122—dc20   91-28236   CIP   AC
Printed in Hong Kong
Set in 16 pt. Caslon 540

Ophelia

On a quiet afternoon, Ophelia B. Clise was tap-tapping on the old typewriter in her shop when she was interrupted by a *boom!* and a *bang!* Sophie and Nou Nou had just come home from school and were behaving rather badly, running and shouting and bumping into customers. Ophelia now knew it was time to talk to these bears about good manners.

After the shop closed, she made a pot of tea, cut slices of chocolate cake, and gathered the bears into a circle to begin the first of many talks about the rules that make living with others more enjoyable.

It's not always easy being a good little bear, but learning about manners can help. Manners are what allows two bears to share a honey sandwich, eight bears to swim in a four-lane pool, and ten bears to get into the same bus without squashing each other. All bears must try to think about how others feel. When they do, they will always practice good manners.

After awhile, Ophelia's lessons made it easier to live in her home. As Sophie and Nou Nou used their manners, even Ricky Jaune, a rackety teenaged bear, caught the spirit. And he cleaned up his room.

Read Ophelia's advice carefully and it could do the same at your home.

Essentials

Please is a very small word with a very great power. It can get you almost anything within reason: Please may I have more chocolate cake? Please may we have a party tomorrow? You may not always get what you want, but at least with "please" you have a better chance.

Good bears try to help each other. But good deeds and kindness must not be taken for granted. Saying "thank you" is simple and easy: Thank you for the cake. Thank you for this party. Always say "please" and "thank you." Please! Thank you!

Schnuffy, Nou Nou, Ophelia, and Sophie

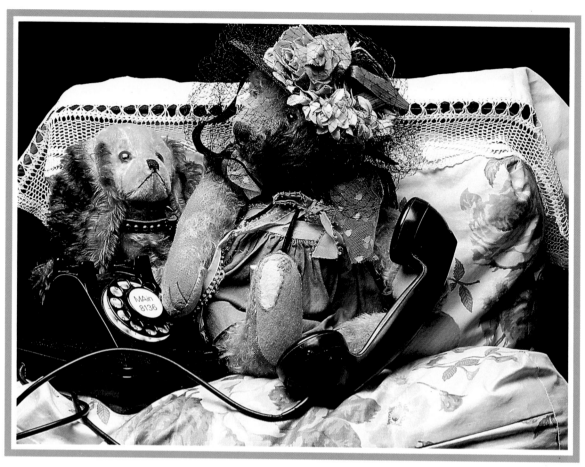

Aunt Vita

When you answer the telephone, politely say hello.
Never shout into the phone, because someone else is at
the other end, even if you can't see them. Ask politely
who is calling, and, if the person they wish to speak to
cannot come to the phone, ask if you can take a
message. Big bears are always pleased when you make it
easier for them to talk to each other.

Poli

Big bears or little bears can make mistakes. You may
have spilled your milk or left your gloves in the park. But
saying you're sorry shows that you regret making anyone
unhappy and will try to be more careful next time.

Table Manners

Good little bears never throw food. Not even when someone else has thrown it first.

Teeny Bears

Teeny Bears ▶

Nou Nou, Ophelia, and Sophie

Napkins keep paws and clothes clean while eating.
Think of them as friends standing between you and the
chocolate cake. You can also use napkins to remove
honey from the end of your nose. Of course, how the
honey got there is another problem entirely.

Ricky Jaune

The more you fidget and make the spaghetti into a pyramid, the more grown-ups will frown and say unpleasant things to you.

It may seem impossible to sit at the dinner table until everyone is finished, but you must try. You can always politely ask to be excused, but if this doesn't work, imagine you're at the ocean on a hot sunny day. Before you know it, it will be time for dessert.

Clarence ▶

Everyday Manners

Everyone likes a neat and tidy bear. Teeth should be brushed, faces washed, and fur combed every day. Soap and water will also prevent any number of unpleasant small creatures from settling into one's fur and producing strange noises and smells that can be very disturbing to those nearby.

Teeny Bears and friends

Nou Nou and friend, Dr. Churchill, and Sophie

Noise disturbs bears all around you. Thoughtful bears
never scream, slam doors, or blow loud horns when
others are trying to rest or work.

Albert and Sophie

Nor is it polite to shout across the room, even if you have something important to say. Always walk over to the bear you want to speak to and talk to them in a regular tone of voice. Shouting only draws attention to yourself and gives a grown-up bear an opportunity to scold you for something you've done and very likely a lot of other things you haven't.

Good little bears go to bed when they are told to. Even though there's always one more chapter of *Winnie-the-Pooh* to read or another somersault to try, smart bears know there is always tomorrow. And smart bears need plenty of sleep if they are to be jolly bears tomorrow.

Poli

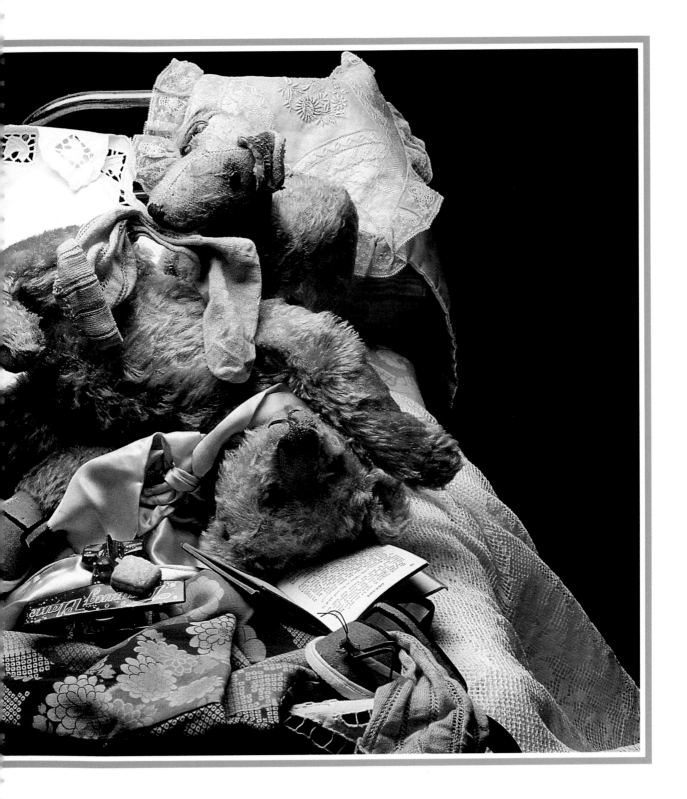

Company Manners

―――― ❧ ――――

Good bears know it's important to
be on time. It's not a good idea to
try to find a long lost sock before
meeting your Aunt Vita for lunch.
She may still be happy to see
you if you're late, but she'll be a
happier bear if you're on time.

Ricky Jaune

Generous bears always share. Never eat all the
candy before other bears have had a chance to enjoy
it too. No one will be impressed that you can eat twenty
chocolate-covered cherries all by yourself.

Brady Boeing and friends

Hats or unusual clothing or mannerisms should not be stared at or remarked upon. The world is made up of all kinds of bears who look and act differently, and you may hurt a bear's feelings if you don't think his shoes are as wonderful as he does.

Albert and friends

Remember to be kind to all creatures great and small
and to take care of our planet. We only have one, and it
and everyone on it appreciate good manners.